JOHN DEERE
CLASSICS

JOHN DEERE
CLASSICS

BY THE AUTO EDITORS OF CONSUMER GUIDE®

Publications International, Ltd.

Louis Weber, CEO
Publications International, Ltd.
7373 North Cicero Avenue
Lincolnwood, Illinois 60712

Permission is never granted for commercial purposes.

ISBN-13: 978-1-4127-1603-1
ISBN-10: 1-4127-1603-9

Manufactured in China.

8 7 6 5 4 3 2 1

Library of Congress Control Number: 2007939130

Credits

Photography:

The editors would like to thank the following people and organizations for supplying the photography that made this book possible. They are listed below, along with the page number(s) of their photos.

Imre Forgo/Dreamstime.com: 128; **Vince Manocchi:** 9-10, 29-30, 33-35, 38, 45-47, 49-51, 53, 57-59, 65-67, 97-99; **Doug Mitchel:** 13-15, 17-19, 21-23, 25, 37, 41-43, 55, 61-63, 69-71, 73-75, 77-79, 81-83, 85-87, 89-91, 93-95, 101-103, 105-107, 109-111, 113-115, 117-119, 121-123, 125-127

Contents: Doug Mitchel
Introduction: Dreamstime.com
Back Cover: Doug Mitchel

Owners:

Special thanks to the owners of the tractors featured in this book for their cooperation. Following are their names and the page number(s) on which their machines appear.

Howard "Shorty" Bonner: 61-63; **H.G. Bouris:** 9-10; **Hershel "Junior" Conway:** 53; **Kenneth Dutenhoeffer:** 49-51; **Pete Dykestra:** 97-99; **Michael Fondren:** 69, back cover; **Ed Frichtl:** 93-95; **Tom Garrison:** 29-30, 45-47; **Randy, Tammy, and Will Germany:** 17-19, 70-71; **Nick Guriel:** 33-35; **Bruce Johnson:** 22-23, 25; **Larry Kindelsperger:** 101-103, 105-107; **Sims McNight:** 13-15, contents; **W. C. "Bill" Milligan:** 65-67; **Jon H. Peterson:** 38; **Paul Sawyer:** 109-111, 113, back cover; **Duane Schlomann:** 21, 23, 55, 73-75, back cover; **Romaine and Kathy Schweer:** 123, 125-127; **Randy and Sharon Sterwald:** 119, back cover; **Billy Surrat:** 114-115; **Danielle Talbott:** 79; **Lance Talbott:** 77-78, 117-118; **Marilynn Talbott:** 37, 89-91; **Ray Volk:** 57-59; **James Welsh:** 85-87; **Stanley White:** 41-43, back cover; **Ed Winkleman:** 121-122; **Gary Winkleman:** 81-83

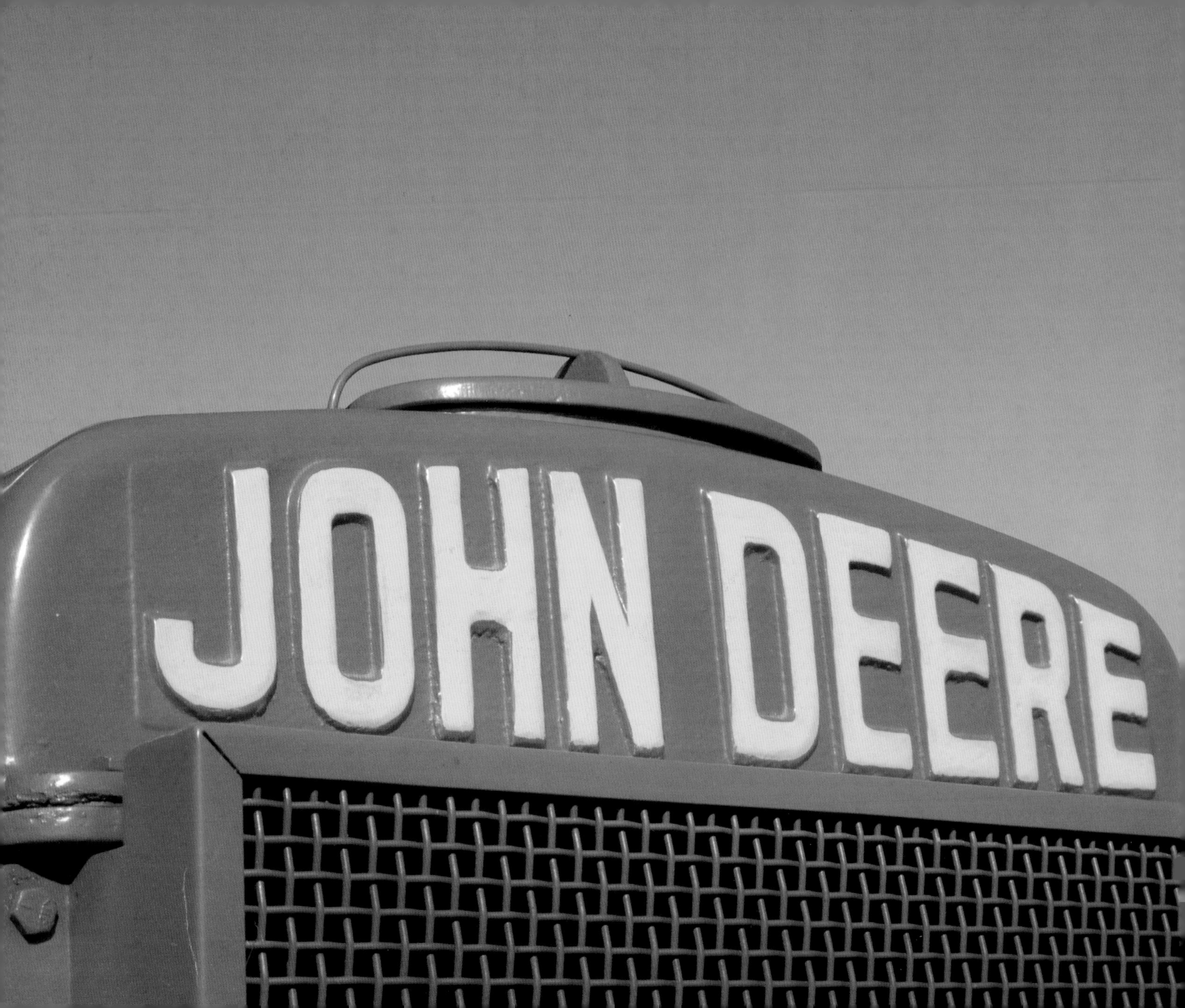
JOHN DEERE

CONTENTS

INTRODUCTION

What began in 1837 with a plow made from a saw blade has since grown into one of the world's foremost manufacturers of farm equipment. "John Deere Green" has become almost a trademark in itself, and the products that wear it have become revered the world over.

For the first 80 years of its existence, John Deere built and sold only implements, leaving the fledgling tractor market to others. But as tractors became more accepted, it was apparent that farmers were looking for equipment compatibility and "one stop shopping."

Although John Deere had already developed its own tractor designs and invested in prototypes, it was decided that buying an already-proven machine and selling it through John Deere dealers would give them an instant product with a strong reputation. To that end, the company purchased the makers of the Waterloo Boy tractor in 1918, and

began advertising and selling the large machine under the John Deere banner.

Deere knew it got a good product out of the Waterloo Boy deal, but what company managers *didn't* know was that along with the big tractor they also got the plans for a smaller tractor already under development. Further refinement to the design resulted in a machine well-suited to medium-sized farms, and it was introduced in 1923 as the first tractor to wear the John Deere name.

Although this book focuses on the glorious tractors that brought mechanization to the nation's farms, let us not forget the hardy souls for whom they were built. A good tractor guided by the able hands of a hard-working farmer is a century-old partnership that has helped feed our nation—and the world.

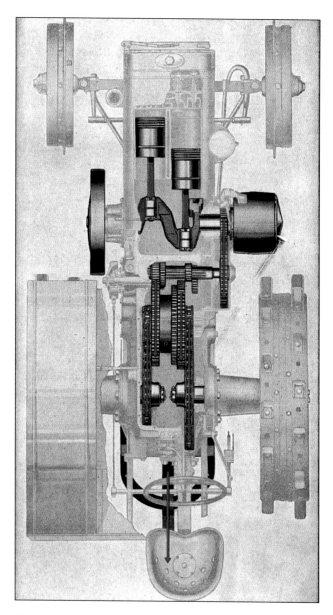

JOHN DEERE'S FIRST TRACTOR
MODEL D

Although small quantities of largely experimental tractors were built earlier by John Deere, the company's first commercially successful tractor was introduced in 1923 as the Model D. And successful it was: Deere sold 23,000 Model Ds in its first five years on the market, and it continued with only minor changes for 15 years before it was "styled"—in which form it continued for *another* 15 years.

The most noteworthy feature of the Model D was its engine—not so much for its technical sophistication or power output as for its historical significance. Its two huge cylinders were laid flat in the frame facing forward, and during two revolutions of the crankshaft (720 degrees), the first cylinder fired at 0 degrees, the second at 180 degrees. Then the crankshaft would rotate 1½ turns (540 degrees) until the first cylinder fired again. Since the "space" between the two firing events was unequal, the engine produced an odd cadence as it ran. Not only would this basic engine con-

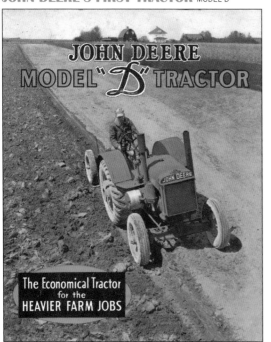

Power to pull a
bottom plow in me
soils and three be
toms under practica
all conditions—pow
to pull a big combi
—power to operate
28-inch thresher
simple, economic
dependable power
every farm job—tha
the famous John De
Model "D" Tractor

From the Atlantic seaboard to the west coast, from the Peace River country in Canada to the Gulf of Mexico, and in all parts of the world where standard tread tractors are used, it is the universal opinion of the many thousands of owners that the John Deere Model "D" Tractor is the leader in all the qualities that mean greater farm profit. Plowing, disking, drilling, planting, combining, and threshing—in all kinds of farm work—these men have found the way to save time, get their work done when conditions are right, and do it at rock-bottom cost.

There are a great many reasons why the John Deere Model "D" is *first* in the qualities you want most.

FIRST IN SIMPLICITY

Only John Deere tractors give you the simplicity of exclusive two-cylinder engine design . . . fewer parts . . . a straight-line transmission without power-consuming bevel gears . . . a belt pulley right on the crankshaft, the simplest construction possible.

- 2 -

10

in all the QUALITIES
that mean GREATER Farm Profit

FIRST IN DEPENDABILITY

Only John Deere two-cylinder tractors give you the dependability of fewer and sturdier parts . . . greater ability to stand up under heavy loads . . . proper distribution of weight for better, more positive traction.

FIRST IN ECONOMY

Only John Deere two-cylinder tractors are backed by a long-time record of success, efficiency and safety in burning the low-cost fuels such as distillate, furnace oil, fuel oil, stove tops, Turner Valley naphtha, and some grades of Diesel oil . . . fuels that cost far less and are approximately 10% more powerful . . . fuels that the John Deere converts into steady, dependable power on drawbar and belt. Burning the low-cost, money-saving fuels in a John Deere tractor is *no experiment.*

But fuel economy is not all. John Deere Model "D" owners also benefit from another great economy . . . the ability to inspect and adjust their tractors right on the farm. The simplicity of two-cylinder design makes possible complete accessibility, one of the big reasons why a recent survey shows that 82% of John Deere owners do fully 75% of their own service work.

EXTRA-LONG LIFE

To the other great features listed, add the extra years of service that the John Deere Model "D" gives, to better understand the big swing to John Deere two-cylinder power. Fewer, heavier, longer-lived parts . . . the use of high-quality materials, careful workmanship, and rigid inspection . . . make records of 8, 10, and even 12 or more years of service not at all unusual.

Low-pressure rubber tires are available for the John Deere Model "D" Tractor when specified.

- 3 -

figuration power most John Deere tractors for the next 35 years, its rhythmic beat prompted admirers to nickname the tractors "Poppin' Johnnies" or "Johnny Poppers," names the two-cylinder tractors are still lovingly known by today.

Early Model Ds can be identified by their six-spoke flywheels, which were replaced by solid flywheels at the end of 1925. The tractor shown here is a 1938 Model D—one of the last unstyled Ds built—but most would be hard-pressed to tell it from one of its earliest ancestors.

The engine initially displaced a whopping 465 cubic inches, good for more than 22 horsepower at the drawbar (indicating how much power was available to pull an implement such as a plow) and 30 horsepower at the pulley (which was used to power machinery). That was enough for the 4000-pound tractor to pull three plows in most soil conditions. The engine was enlarged to 501 cubic inches for 1928, by which time it produced 28 horsepower at the drawbar, 36 at the pulley. By the end of the unstyled era, it was up to nearly 31 at the drawbar, and more than 41 at the pulley.

FRANK TRAVER
Clinton, Ia., • • • •
in the field with his
John Deere Model D
Tractor *and* John Deere
No. 5 Three-Bottom Plow

MONEY-MAKING POWER
For ALL Your Farm Jobs

Regardless of your crops or your acreage, regardless of your power requirements, you can now get John Deere power that will do all your farm work with satisfaction and profit to you.

For the Heavier Farm Jobs

On thousands of farms where big capacity and speed in the field and on the belt are necessary to a profitable farming program, the *John Deere Model D* is a money-maker.

Here is more than power to pull three or four plows, to pull a 28" separator—to do all the many other heavier farm jobs. The Model D combines with its great capacity all the other things that give you balanced performance.

Its light weight permits its use in fields and under conditions that keep the heavier tractors idle. And light weight, combined with fewer friction-making parts, reduces the loss of power to a minimum.

The Model D delivers an extremely high percentage of its engine power to the drawbar and belt. This is one of the reasons why, per acre or per day, cost of fuel and oil is astonishingly low.

Built to the John Deere high standard of quality—good materials, advanced design, careful workmanship—with all parts enclosed and running in a bath of oil—the Model D is giving extra years of low-cost service.

For the Row Crop Farmer

The farmer who diversifies can now use mechanical power to cut production costs—to increase his daily capacity—to reduce labor costs. *The John Deere General Purpose Tractor,* of standard design, plants and cultivates three rows at a time, pulls a two-bottom plow; in fact, does all farm jobs within its power range equally well.

Special equipment, including three-row planter, three-row cultivator, power-driven mower, power-lift sweep rake, besides the complete line of John Deere power-operated machinery, is available.

Four sources of power—drawbar, belt, power take-off *and* power lift—adapt this General Purpose tractor to every field or belt job you may have for it.

For the row crop farmer, here is ideal power. It gives you power farming in full measure.

Interesting Booklets Free For the Asking

Be sure to get our latest booklets on these tractors. Write today and ask for booklets RE-15. Also, see your John Deere dealer. Equip your farm with John Deere power and get the extra profit that is sure to follow.

The
JOHN DEERE
General Purpose
Tractor

Plants corn uniformly and accurately in big volume—30 to 40 acres a day. Planter forms unit with tractor. Power lift raises and lowers runners—no levers to operate.

Millard Oppedike, Joslin, Illinois, farmer (above), planted and cultivated 400 acres of corn in 1928 with his John Deere General Purpose Tractor. Big capacity—25 to 40 acres a day. No levers—a power lift, the fourth source of power, does the work.

Pulls a two-bottom plow with two wheels in furrow, and a straight center-hitch for plow and tractor. Easy to guide—no side draft.

1930
MODEL GP

John Deere's first tractor, the Model D, was considered a fairly heavy-duty tractor for its day. Its 4000-pound heft, 30 horsepower at the pulley, and low, wide stance made it perfect for plowing large fields and operating threshing machines off its pulley.

But not every farmer needed such a large tractor, and, in fact, those who had them often found it necessary to use horses for more delicate work such as planting and cultivating. As a result, John Deere brought out the smaller Model C in 1927, which was renamed the Model GP (General Purpose) the following year.

The GP weighed in at about 3600 pounds, and its engine produced about 20 horsepower at the pulley.

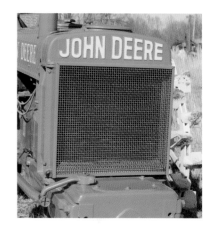

In addition to the pulley, it offered a power take-off (PTO) for running implements.

Due to its lighter weight and lower cost, the GP sold in far greater numbers than the D and really helped put John Deere on the map. It was soon available with a narrow or wide front track, and it became the first John Deere to offer Power Lift, a power equipment lift. Initial models were fitted with traditional steel wheels as shown here; the factory didn't make pneumatic (rubber) tires available until the early 1930s.

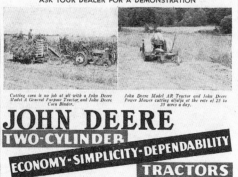
1935
MODEL A

As tractors became more accepted, they also became more diverse. Some were developed to be better-suited to specific tasks, and the Model A that arrived in 1934 is a good example.

The Model A is considered a "row crop" tractor, as its front wheels are close together and angled slightly (to go between two rows) and its rear wheels can slide in and out on their axles so they can be adjusted to straddle rows of various widths. In size, weight, and power, the A was larger than the GP, which evolved into the Model B. The A weighed about 3800 pounds and was rated at 24 horsepower at the pulley.

Whereas most GPs had a steering column that angled down toward the engine, the A's column ran almost horizontally above the hood to a vertical steering post. The Model B, which arrived shortly after the A, had the same arrangement. They differ, however, in that on the A, the cover at the top of the post is smooth in front with four bolts on the back; on the B, the cover has two bolts on the front. The Model A has the

distinction of being—by a narrow margin—the most popular
two-cylinder tractor ever sold by John Deere.

One of the major innovations for tractors arrived in the
early 1930s in the form of pneumatic rubber tires. Tests
showed these "air" tires transferred more power to the ground
than steel wheels. But even more important to farmers was
the fact they provided a far smoother ride, and also allowed
the tractors to be driven on streets, which meant they could
be used to pull wagons into town.

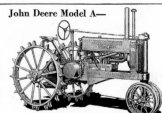
1935-36
MODEL B

Introduced for the 1935 model year, the Model B effectively replaced the Model GP, which had been around since 1928. The Model B weighed about 2800 pounds and was rated at 18 horsepower at the pulley.

Like its bigger Model A brother, the B was offered as a row-crop tractor, with its front wheels close together and its rear wheels able to be moved in and out on the axle to vary the distance between them. The design allowed the front wheels to go between narrow rows, the rear wheels to straddle rows of different widths. The B was also offered with wide-spaced front wheels, which, like the rears, could be adjusted in and out to vary the track width.

On the very first Model Bs, the steering post was attached to the frame with four bolts; soon after, eight bolts were used. As a result, four-bolt models are very rare and quite valuable. During its life span, which extended through 1952, the Model B sold only slightly fewer copies than John Deere's best-selling two-cylinder tractor, the Model A.

1938
MODEL B

In late 1937, the Model B was given a longer frame that allowed it to share more parts with the larger Model A, thus cutting production costs. In collector circles, these later Bs are known as "long frame" versions.

Model Bs were offered with a variety of front-end designs. "Wide-tread" models (denoted with a "W" in the model name, such as "BW") had the front wheels far apart, while "tricycle" versions had them close together (also called "Narrow tread," which prompted an "N" in the model designation). A variation of the tricycle had a single front wheel, as shown here. Some models of both Wide and Narrow configuration were mounted higher off the ground for more crop clearance, and these added an "H" to their model name.

One of the selling points of the Model B was its fuel economy, much of which was attributable to its two-cylinder design. (Many competitors used thirstier four-cylinder engines.) Another was that some versions could be run on low-grade fuels such as distillate and furnace oil, which cost less than gasoline. Since fuel made up a large part of a farmer's budget, these were important considerations—something ads of the day clearly pointed out. Also mentioned were individual brakes on the rear wheels that allowed for tighter turning and a hydraulic power lift for implements.

In 1931, it was estimated that only one farmer in six owned a tractor, despite studies that showed tractors cost less than horses to maintain. But as the Depression eased in the mid-1930s and tractor costs came down, more and more farmers made the switch. With its low price, low operating costs, convenient features, and strong reputation, the Model B was a popular first tractor for farmers who were "moving up" from horses.

1941
MODEL B

After the advent of pneumatic tires in the early 1930s, the next great leap in tractor development came with the "styled" tractors that arrived later that same decade. In the case of John Deere, most of the changes can be attributed to industrial designer Henry Dreyfuss. Dreyfuss did not work for Deere, but rather had his own design firm and operated out of New York.

The first styled John Deere tractors appeared for the 1939 model year. Sheetmetal surrounded the radiator, flowed into the side panels, and enclosed the top-mounted steering column, providing a sleek, more modern look. Styled Model Bs were given seven radiator slots, and their exhaust stack sprouted from the hood just ahead of the air-cleaner stack.

However, the beauty of these tractors was more than skin deep. Ergonomics (the relation between seat, steering wheel, pedals, and controls) were also improved, which—along with the "cushy" pneumatic tires—greatly increased operator comfort and productivity.

Despite the advantages in both appearance and comfort, not all John Deere tractors got styled. An ad from the early 1940s shows that several models, including the big Model G row-crop tractor and the Orchard variants, escaped Dreyfuss's touch. Also shown is the depth and variation of the John Deere lineup at this point, with sizes and styles to meet almost any farming need.

1941
MODEL H

In an effort to appeal to farmers for whom even the Model B was a financial stretch, John Deere brought out the Model H in 1939. It arrived in styled form and looked much like a scaled-down B. It had seven grille slots (like the B), but only the exhaust pipe poked up from the top of the hood; the air cleaner was housed behind a small, mesh screen on the left side-panel, just ahead of the John Deere logo.

Weighing in at 2063 pounds, the Model H was about 700 pounds lighter than a Model B. It also had a much smaller engine: 100 cubic inches vs. 149, which would prove to be the smallest horizontal twin John Deere ever built. It was rated at 12.5 horsepower at the drawbar,

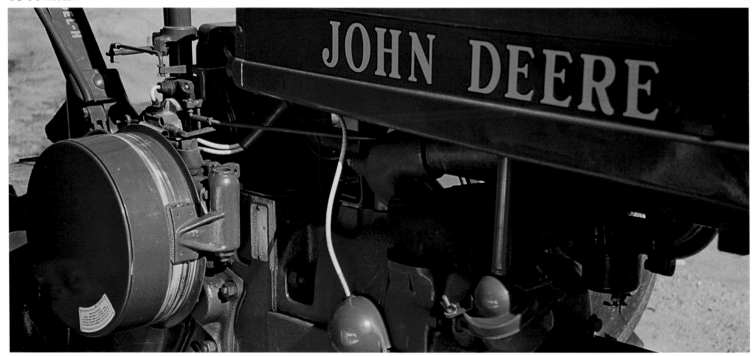

15 at the pulley. John Deere called the Model H a "one-to-two-plow" tractor, which slotted it between the little one-plow Model L and the two-plow Model B. (The larger Model A was rated for two-to-three plows, the big Model G for three plows.)

In addition to its "first-time buyer" audience, the Model H was also marketed as a light-duty workhorse on farms that already had a larger tractor. Ads promoted both uses, noting that the Model H "handles all jobs on the small farm, replaces the last team [of horses] on the large one." Indeed, some farms that were "mechanized" at the time still used horse-drawn equipment for some tasks—but that was quickly changing.

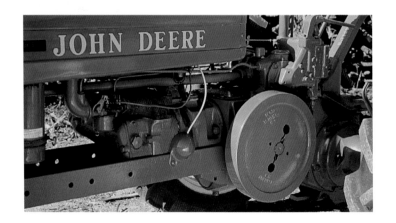

1941 MODEL L AND
1946 MODEL LA

The smallest tractor John Deere offered during the "Two-Cylinder" era was introduced in 1937 as the Model 62, but was renamed the Model L later that same year. It was powered by a vertical two-cylinder engine built by Hercules that developed seven horsepower at the drawbar, 10 at the pulley, enough to warrant a one-plow rating. Weighing in at just 1515 pounds, it featured a foot-operated clutch (most Deere clutches were operated with a hand lever) and individual rear brakes that allowed a seven-foot turning radius, making it perfect for use in tight quarters.

Styled sheetmetal was applied to the Model L in 1939, and it got a Deere-built engine with the same power rating for 1941. It was joined that same

year by the slightly larger LA (shown above), which looked nearly identical but tipped the scales at 2200 pounds, and its larger engine produced 13 horsepower at the drawbar, 14 at the pulley. Production ceased on the L and LA midway through 1946, and no successor replaced them in the lineup.

1943
MODEL A

Like the smaller Model B, John Deere's Model A became "styled" for 1939. Also like the B, the process brought sleeker lines headed by a sheetmetal grille, but in this case, the grille had eight slots instead of seven. (The larger Model G also had eight, but the two can be told apart because the G had its air-cleaner and exhaust stacks side-by-side, whereas the A had them one behind the other, like the B.)

Despite the obvious appearance improvements, ads of the day continued to stress the low cost of John Deere ownership. "Upkeep is mighty low," one states, and "The John Deere is the simplest tractor built … But where you will notice the big saving is in fuel costs." Both benefits were credited to the tractor's two-cylinder engine, a design Deere had been building for 20 years.

By this time, the Model A was rated at 26 horsepower at the

drawbar, nearly 30 at the pulley. The two figures were much closer than they had been 15 years earlier (see the 1930 GP) due to advances in driveline technology that reduced power loss. Also, "pulley horsepower" was becoming a dated term; most tractors could be ordered with a power take-off (PTO), and that was rapidly becoming the standard way to drive equipment—and measure horsepower.

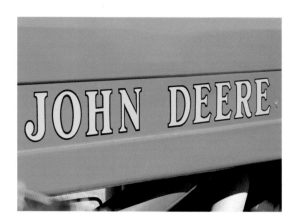

For Lower Cost Orchard Work

The New John Deere AO Orchard Tractor stands only 55 inches high at the radiator cap.

Getting under the low-hanging branches, up close to trees with the John Deere CH Disk Harrow.

A John Deere Orchard Tractor and John Deere No. 3 Cultivator keeps this orchard in good tilth.

When you put a John Deere Orchard Tractor and tillage equipment to work, your costs go down.

Costs go down because with their exclusive two-cylinder engine design, John Deere tractors are built for long life. They burn low-cost fuels. They are simpler—easier to maintain, to keep in perfect running order.

Specially designed with individually-operated differential brakes, you can make unusually short turns at the head lands. Built low, you can slip under low-hanging branches—get up close to trees.

Like John Deere Tractors, John Deere Tillage Implements are also built to last longer, to handle easier, to cut your costs—increase your profits.

Get the whole story. The coupon below brings it. Or, see your John Deere dealer.

1944
MODEL AO

Shortly after the 1934 introduction of the Model A row-crop tractor, John Deere brought out a version specially suited for use in orchards. It was—quite appropriately—designated the Model AO.

Visually distinctive features of the AO were its standard-tread (wide) front axle that permitted a low ground clearance, stubby air-cleaner and exhaust stacks, and wide, sweeping rear fenders; fenders that fully enclosed the rear wheels were also available (see ad at left). All these modifications were made to avoid "catching" low-hanging branches.

Also featured on the AO were individual rear brakes. These al-

lowed the operator to brake just the inside wheel during a turn, which made for a tighter turning radius—useful when trying to maneuver around closely spaced trees.

The AO was one of the few John Deere tractors that didn't get "styled" in the late 1930s or early '40s. Instead, it soldiered on in unstyled form, as shown on the featured 1944 version.

for Every Farm ...
for Every Crop ...
for Every Purpose

2 SIZES 2 MODELS
GROVE AND ORCHARD

3 SIZES 3 MODELS
STANDARD TREAD TRACTORS

GENERAL PURPOSE TRACTORS
5 SIZES 14 MODELS

AMONG the nineteen John Deere Tractors there is the size and type to meet your customers' needs exactly. And available for each is a remarkably complete line of equipment to handle all work easier, better, with greater satisfaction.

And, burning the low-cost fuels efficiently, safely, and successfully, John Deere Tractors enable farmers to do more work for every dollar they spend for fuel—the basis of *true* fuel economy.

In addition to this economy of fuel consumption, John Deere Tractors provide also the economy of longer tractor life, of fewer, sturdier parts, of easy, simple maintenance—the line of tractors with the BIG FOUR your customers want—Economy, Dependability, Adaptability, and Easy Handling.

JOHN DEERE
Moline, Illinois

JOHN DEERE *Two-Cylinder* TRACTORS
FOR ECONOMY ... SIMPLICITY ... DEPENDABILITY ... EASE OF HANDLING

1946
MODEL D

John Deere's big bruiser, the Model D, enjoyed the longest production run in the company's history. From its introduction in 1923 as the first tractor to wear the John Deere name to its final edition 30 years later, the Model D changed surprisingly little.

One area in which it did change was in appearance. Like many other models in the line, the Model D received stylish sheetmetal for the 1939 model year. Unlike the others, however, its new grille featured vertical slots rather than horizontal "gills," which instantly set it apart.

What didn't change—even with the new look—was the D's chunky, massive character. It was lower and much shorter than the row-crop Model A, yet also significantly heavier. With its huge 501-cubic-inch two-cylinder engine, the Model D was rated at nearly 31 horsepower at the drawbar and 38 at the pulley running on kerosene, and tipped the scales at a hefty 5300 pounds. None of these

figures seem very impressive by today's standards, but by an early postwar yardstick, they were brutish.

A diesel-powered version of the Model D was introduced for 1949 as the Model R. It was even heavier and put out more horsepower, marking the first time the Model D wasn't the king of the John Deere hill.

The assembly line churned out its last Model D in March 1953, but that wasn't the end of production. Several more were handbuilt at a location away from the factory using spare parts. Like other tractors in the John Deere line, the Model D's redesigned successor received a numeric designation, arriving in late 1953 as the Model 80.

John Deere Model "AO"
Grove and Orchard Tractor

The John Deere Model "AO" Grove and Orchard Tractor has the pulling capacity of a 6-horse team, and the daily work output of 8 horses. At its highest point, the top of the cowl, this tractor stands only 53 inches high. Ideal for orchards, groves, vineyards, hopyards.

John Deere Models "AO" and "BO" Grove and Orchard Tractors

ONE glance at a John Deere Model "AO" Grove and Orchard Tractor and you know that here is a tractor specially designed for orchard work . . . built low and completely streamlined to save trees and fruit.

One trip into the orchard and you are more convinced. Short turns around trees, four forward speeds, built-in power shaft, easy handling . . . these are all important features.

One day's work and you *know* that the John Deere is the tractor you want. John Deere economy wins again.

Both the fully streamlined Model "AO", and the slightly less streamlined Model "BO", are built low and are fully protected to avoid catching branches. Citrus fenders are special equipment. On rubber-tired models, solid cast wheels eliminate all rear-wheel spokes and, in most cases, make wheel weights unnecessary. Both tractors work in close to trees, even though branches are trimmed low.

Easy Handling in Tight Quarters

Due to automotive-type steering, and independently operated differential brakes, you can make extremely short turns around trees and at the ends of tree rows. There's plenty of room for the operator on the platform, and the seat is so located that the operator's head is only a little above the steering wheel.

Handle Many Jobs

Four speeds forward—2, 3, 4, and 6-1/4 miles per hour—adapt these tractors to a wide variety of uses including hauling. There is a reverse of 3 miles per hour. You'll find these tractors efficient power plants for both field and belt work. In plowing, you have a center hitch to both plow and tractor, with two wheels in the furrow.

John Deere Models "AO" and "BO" Tractors have all the mechanical advantages that make John Deere tractors so economical, so dependable, so adaptable, so outstanding.

John Deere Model "BO"
Grove and Orchard Tractor

Standing only 52 inches high, the John Deere Model "BO" Grove and Orchard Tractor handles the load of a 4-horse team, and provides the sustained work output of 6 horses. It is shown at right with steel wheels which are regular equipment, and with special citrus fenders which are extra. Can also be furnished with low-pressure rubber tires and solid cast wheels as shown on the Model "AO" Tractor, above, at extra cost.

1947
MODEL BO

As had its Model A counterpart, the Model B was offered in a specially designed version for use in orchards. Called the Model BO, it featured many of the alterations of its AO sibling, including a low ride height, ultra-short air cleaner and exhaust stacks, and encompassing rear fenders, all in the interest of avoiding damage to low-hanging branches. Also available were fully skirted rear fenders as shown at the bottom of the ad at left.

Like the AO, the BO had individual rear brakes that allowed the operator to brake just the inside wheel for tighter turns in the confined space of an orchard. Also like the AO, the BO didn't get the late-'30s styling treatment applied to most other models in the John Deere line, instead remaining in unstyled form through the end of its production run.

An interesting variation of the Model BO was a tracked crawler built by Lindeman, a company other-wise not associated with John Deere. On Lindeman versions, the steering wheel was replaced by a pair of control levers. These activated track clutches that would transfer power to one side or the other, causing the tractor to turn—a system similar to that used on tanks. John Deere purchased Lindeman in the late 1940s, and soon came out with its own crawler based on the upcoming Model 40.

1948
MODEL A

After getting styled for 1939, the Model A received a Powr-Trol hydraulic system in late 1945. Powr-Trol powered a hydraulic lift cylinder and allowed precise positioning of a towed implement.

The next big step in the evolution of the Model A occurred in 1947, and this general design would carry through to the end of production. Most noticeable was the new pressed-steel frame, which made these models instantly identifiable due to a "kick up" just behind the

grille that covered the side of the engine. A padded seat was also available, and the battery was placed beneath it.

A slightly larger 332-cubic-inch engine with standard electric starting was fitted to these "late" Model As, and horsepower was measured at 38 at the pulley/PTO—quite a step up from the 16 horsepower produced by the earliest versions. But weight had also increased substantially since the model's introduction in 1934, nearly doubling to about 6000 pounds.

1949
MODEL R

When it was introduced for the 1949 model year, the diesel-powered Model R replaced the venerable Model D as top dog in the John Deere line. Its big 415-cubic-inch diesel engine continued the Deere tradition of horizontally mounted twin cylinders, and put out 45 horsepower vs. 38 for the kerosene-burning Model D.

Since diesel engines were notoriously hard to start—particularly in cold temperatures—the R was fitted with a small, two-cylinder, gasoline-powered "pup" motor that was mounted near the flywheel and used for starting. The pup motor had an electric starter, and once running, it could warm the diesel engine and then turn it over.

Aside from its engine, the Model R was much like the Model D. Both came in only one configuration, with standard tread and a low ride

height. The R was the first Deere model to offer an all-steel cab, along with "live" (meaning it was powered directly off the engine) PTO and hydraulics.

As it turned out, the Model R's reign was rather short. Along with most other "Letter Series" tractors, it lasted only through 1953, after which it was reborn as the Model 80—which likewise topped the line.

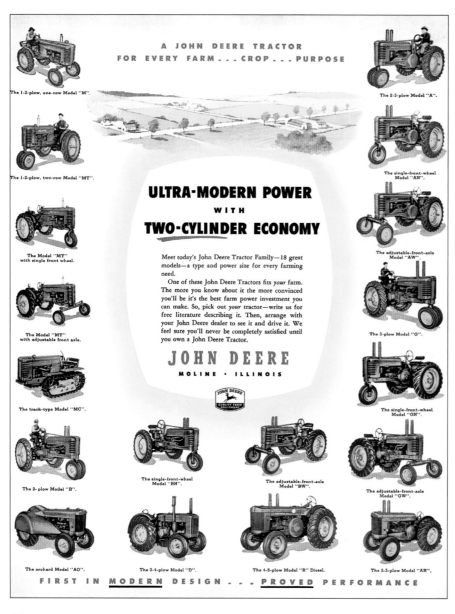

A JOHN DEERE TRACTOR
FOR EVERY FARM...CROP...PURPOSE

The 1-2-plow, one-row Model "M".

The 1-2-plow, two-row Model "MT".

The Model "MT" with single front wheel.

The Model "MT" with adjustable front axle.

The track-type Model "MC".

The 2-plow Model "B".

The orchard Model "AO".

The 3-4-plow Model "D".

The single-front-wheel Model "BN".

The adjustable-front-axle Model "BW".

The 4-5-plow Model "R" Diesel.

The 2-3-plow Model "A".

The single-front-wheel Model "AN".

The adjustable-front-axle Model "AW".

The 3-plow Model "G".

The single-front-wheel Model "GN".

The adjustable-front-axle Model "GW".

The 2-3-plow Model "AR".

ULTRA-MODERN POWER
WITH
TWO-CYLINDER ECONOMY

Meet today's John Deere Tractor Family—18 great models—a type and power size for every farming need.

One of these John Deere Tractors fits *your* farm. The more you know about it the more convinced you'll be it's the best farm power investment you can make. So, pick out *your* tractor—write us for free literature describing it. Then, arrange with your John Deere dealer to see it and drive it. We feel sure you'll never be completely satisfied until you own a John Deere Tractor.

JOHN DEERE
MOLINE · ILLINOIS

FIRST IN MODERN DESIGN ... PROVED PERFORMANCE

1950
MODEL M

Like its Model L and LA predecessors, the Model M of 1947 departed from usual John Deere practice in having its two-cylinder engine standing upright, mounted longitudinally in the frame; all other Deeres since the company's beginning had their engines laid flat with cylinders facing forward. The M also used the engine as a structural member, making it a "unit design."

Several new features marked the Model M. The padded seat included inflatable cushions and was adjustable fore and aft, while the steering wheel could be telescoped through a one-foot range, allowing the driver to either stand or sit.

Originally introduced with a standard front end, the Model MT (for Tricycle) was added in 1949; two-wheeled tricycle and wide front ends appeared at the same time. MTs also boasted dual hydraulics, which allowed separate lift controls for the left and right side. And a new system

of attaching implements greatly decreased the amount of time it took to connect and disconnect them.

A 101-cubic-inch engine delivered about 14 drawbar horsepower and just under 20 at the belt pulley. Although the one-plow-rated tractor was well-suited to smaller farms, it remained in the line only until 1952.

There's a feeling of genuine satisfaction in owning a John Deere Tractor. You experience it one way or another every day you're at the wheel.

The extra lugging ability at plowing time ... the way Roll-O-Matic literally paves the way over rough ground ... the unexcelled view when cultivating ... the light touch that releases hydraulic Powr-Trol to operate drawn and integral tools ... the extreme comfort and convenience that lessen fatigue —these are just a few of the pleasant daily reminders that you're driving a John Deere.

Best of all, owner satisfaction grows with the years as the matchless simplicity, ruggedness, and totally-different design of John Deere *Two-Cylinder* Tractors pays off in *lower* operating and maintenance costs ... in *greater* dependability ... *longer* life ... *better* all-around field performance.

Try the size and type that fits your farm and you, too, will want to join the great family of enthusiastic John Deere Tractor owners.

JOHN ✶ DEERE

Moline, Illinois

Full 3-plow power for large row-crop farms.

Ideal 2-plow power for medium size farms.

The powerful 3-plow tractor that burns heavier fuels.

JOHN DEERE, Moline, Ill.
Send free literature on John Deere General-Purpose Tractors.

Name

Town

State

JOHN DEERE
Two-Cylinder
TRACTORS
FIRST IN **MODERN** DESIGN AND **PROVED** PERFORMANCE

1950-51
MODEL G

John Deere introduced the Model G in 1937 as its largest row-crop tractor. Weighing in at 4400 pounds, it was powered by a 413-cubic-inch two-cylinder engine that provided 36 horsepower at the pulley.

Early versions of the Model G were unstyled—that is, with no sheetmetal covering the radiator or steering gear—and the G was among the last in the line to get the "styled" treatment.

Styled versions, introduced in 1942, were briefly called the Model GM; this because the government dictated a "price freeze" during World War II, and the new sheetmetal kicked up the cost. Deere got around the policy by changing the model name, but reverted back to "Model G" after the war.

Like John Deere's smaller Model A row-crop tractor, the Model G's grille had eight slots on each side of the

central steering-gear cover. However, whether styled or unstyled, the Model G had its air-cleaner stack and exhaust stack opposite each other on either side of the hood (on the Model A, they were behind one another in the center of the hood), making them easy to spot. Also like the Model A, the G was described in advertising as a "3-plow" tractor, but those plows could be 16-inchers rather than 14s.

As were Deere's other "letter series" tractors, the Model G was redesigned for 1953 and given a numeric designation; in this case, the Model 70. It then evolved into the 720, and later, the beloved 730.

1952
MODEL A

During its 20-year life span, numerous versions of John Deere's venerable Model A were offered, which helped cement its position as the best-selling tractor in the company's history.

One of the more unusual configurations was the Hi-Crop version. The example pictured was originally shipped to California for use in gladiola fields.

Raising the front end off the ground was fairly easy, but raising the rear required special gearboxes that were fitted between the axle and the wheel hub. Easing entry to the elevated helm were step-plate "stairs" mounted to the left-rear axle housing.

When the Model A was finally retired in 1953, it was succeeded in the line by the Model 60, which didn't enjoy anywhere near as long a life.

1953
MODEL 40

What appeared in 1947 as the Model M evolved into the Model 40 when redesigned for 1953. Most other models in the line were also new, and all adopted numeric designations. Revised styling incorporated vertical-slot grilles that mimicked that of the big Model R introduced in 1949. Those with a tricycle front end retained a sheet-metal "spine" running down the center of the grille.

With the demise of the Model L and LA in 1946, the Model M had become John Deere's smallest offering, and the 40 carried on that role. Retained on the 40 was the M's vertical two-cylinder engine that defied John Deere's tradition of horizontal twins. Though still sized at 101 cubic inches, output increased by about four horsepower to 22 at the drawbar, 24 at the pulley/PTO.

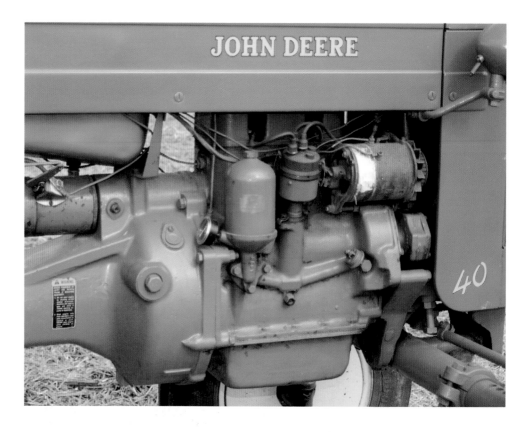

Like the Model M, the 40 was of "unit" design, with the engine and transmission cases serving as the frame to which the front and rear ends were attached. Revised styling made the 40 look huskier than its M predecessor, more in keeping with its 4000-pound heft. New was a padded seat to replace the former steel seat pan.

Deere's smallest tractor came in a wide variety of configurations and offered numerous features. Tricycle, standard, and low-slung utility front ends were available, along with a crawler version. A three-point hitch was added, as was Touch-O-Matic hydraulics, all of which made the Model 40 surprisingly versatile.

1954
MODEL 60

John Deere's popular Model A was redesigned and given the Model 60 designation for 1953. Grille slots switched from horizontal to vertical, and only tricycle versions retained a center sheetmetal cover for the steering post. Other easily recognized changes included a new frame design that increased overall length, and a padded seat to replace the steel seat pan.

Further revisions appeared on the mechanical side. A six-speed transmission replaced a four-speed, and dual carburetors helped boost horsepower a bit, now rated at nearly 37 horsepower at the drawbar, 41 at the pulley/PTO.

Also offered was a "live" PTO run off the engine rather than the transmission, and Quick-Change,

which allowed faster adjustment of rear tread width. Row-crop versions were available with Roll-O-Matic front end, which forced one front wheel down when the other encountered a bump, thereby helping to maintain stability, and later models were offered with power steering and a three-point hitch.

Unlike its vaunted Model A predecessor, the Model 60 didn't last long on the market—though that wasn't due to any failings of the tractor itself. Another round of revisions soon prompted another change in designations, and the Model 60 evolved into the Model 620 for 1957.

Whether you grow grain or row crops on a large scale, John Deere offers you the *big power* you need to make your operations more profitable. It's power that's amazingly economical — that will do more work on a given amount of fuel — that will cost far less to maintain through the years.

Until you've tried a John Deere Model "R" Diesel and measured its *unequalled* fuel economy, you've no idea how much better, easier, and more profitable grain farming can be. Here's husky *two-cylinder* power that handles a 4- or 5-bottom plow and similar big-capacity equipment in practically any condition . . . five modern speeds, "live" power shaft and hydraulic Powr-trol, automotive-type steering, plus the kind of operating economy that can cut several hundred dollars off your annual fuel bill.

What the "R" is to the grain grower, the new John Deere Model "70" is to the large row-crop farmer. It's the 4-5-plow tractor specifically designed to handle every tillage, planting, cultivating, haying, and harvesting job easier, faster, better than ever before. In addition to gasoline and tractor fuel, the "70" can be equipped *at the factory* for LP-Gas. It's available with a "live" power shaft, offers "live" Powr-trol and many, many other features as regular equipment.

Your John Deere dealer has all the facts on the powerful, economical "R" Diesel and Model "70" Tractors. See him without delay.

Send for Free Literature

JOHN DEERE

1956
MODEL 70

A successor to the Model G appeared in 1953, and like other models in the John Deere line, it carried a numeric designation: the Model 70.

In keeping with John Deere's commitment to giving the buyer choices, the 70 was available with standard-tread or row-crop front ends. Early models were offered in versions that ran on gasoline, all-fuel (which was similar to gasoline but cheaper), or Liquid Propane Gas (LPG). All these engines used a new two-barrel carburetor, and the LPG version had aluminum pistons and a stronger crankshaft to handle the engine's higher compression. For 1954, a diesel-powered 70 was added to the roster. Regardless of the fuel, the 70 delivered almost 20 percent more horsepower than the Model G.

Unlike other Deeres of the day, the Model 70's six-speed transmission was shifted with two levers rather than just one. Power steering was now optional, and versions so equipped could be identified by their three-spoke steering wheel (others had a four-spoke wheel) and "Power Steering" decal on the side of the grille. Also located there was the model identification (in this case, "70"), which was helpful in that some of the early number-series Deeres were otherwise difficult to tell apart.

All of the early (two digit) number-series tractors had a rather short life. For 1957, the 70 would be replaced by the updated 720.

1956
MODEL 420

For 1956, the Model 40 was updated to become the Model 420, appearing in late 1955 as the first of the "three digit" Deeres. (Most of its siblings didn't arrive until mid-1956.) Unlike the 40, the 420 would not be the "baby" of the John Deere family.

Due to a 20 percent boost in horsepower—largely the result of a displacement increase for its vertical two-cylinder engine to 113.3 cubic inches—a space opened up for a lower-powered model. John Deere filled the gap with the Model 320, which in many ways could be considered the successor to the Model M, last sold in the early '50s.

The Model 420 was offered with narrow and wide front ends, along with a tracked crawler version that replaced the former Lindeman-built crawlers. Engines ran on gasoline or all-fuel, and an LPG version appeared for 1958, the 420's final year.

The first 420s were painted all green; later versions

added yellow trim as seen here. New were an optional five-speed transmission and "live" (engine driven) PTO. For 1958, the steering wheels of most versions were mounted at an angle, which many operators found more convenient than the vertical mounting of earlier models.

1957
MODEL 720

John Deere's 20-series tractors that arrived for 1957 offered buyers a wide range of models, but most were similar to those they replaced. The 720 took over for the Model 70 in the line.

A new engine in the 720 produced 20 percent more horsepower than that in the Model 70 for a total of 59. An LPG-fueled version was offered, as shown here; the telltale sign is the huge barrel-shaped tank just ahead of the steering wheel. A single shift lever replaced the dual-stick arrangement of the 70, and first gear on the 720 was now considered a "creeper" gear. Optional gearing available for 1958 increased top speed to eight mph.

Other optional equipment for the 720 included power steering and Float Ride seat with foam rubber cushion.

A vertical intake stack and rear-facing exhaust were two more choices, and Custom Powr-Trol now included a true three-point hitch, along with the capability of powering two remote hydraulic cylinders. As before, narrow-tread versions offered the Roll-O-Matic front end, which forced one wheel down when the other went over a bump, aiding stability and helping to smooth the ride.

Despite its popularity, the 720 was built in 1957 and 1958 only. In late 1958, it was replaced by an equally short-lived "30 series" tractor, the 730.

JOHN DEERE TRACTOR POWER Opens the Door to

Modern Methods ...Greater Profits

One Man, One Outfit, in One Trip *cuts and conditions hay with the fast-working John Deere "520" Tractor, Power Mower, and Hay Conditioner. Conditioned hay makes better feed, cures in half the time, and insures against crop losses. The tractor's new Independent PTO drives both machines.*

Fast, Nimble 2-3 Plow "420" Power *handles many big-tractor jobs at big money savings. This low-cost Row-Crop Utility is one of six wheel types. Available with continuous-running PTO and 5-speed transmission. Shown here pulling and operating a John Deere 14-T Twine-Tie Baler.*

Championship Fuel Economy *is one of many outstanding features of this powerful 5-6 Plow "820" Diesel—the tractor that slashes labor and operating costs on large-acreage grain and rice farms. Here, it is pulling two John Deere "LZ-A" Grain Drills. Twin remote cylinders raise and lower the drills individually or simultaneously.*

You'll step up your farming operations, increase your earnings and savings in many new ways, with a modern John Deere Tractor on your farm.

Here is **new power** that will turn out more work for you per day . . . **new adaptability** to handle more of your jobs more conveniently than ever before . . . **new comfort and handling ease** to save you physical effort and relieve driver fatigue.

Get Behind the Wheel

But John Deere Tractor Power in action speaks louder than any words. So, pay a visit to your dealer and arrange for a field demonstration of the model that fits your requirements. Get behind the wheel yourself and "give it the works." Make any comparisons you want to make and you'll come up with one answer: *"It's a John Deere Tractor for me."*

Today's Most Powerful Row-Crop Tractor—*the new 5-plow "720"—replaces two tractors on many farms at tillage time. Shown here with the famous 490 Corn Planter and new Liquid Fertilizer Attachment.*

Unmatched Handling Ease and Comfort *step up work capacity, greatly reduce driver fatigue. Individual or simultaneous control of right, left, and rear cultivator units . . . effortless power steering that saves muscle every minute of every job . . . knee-action front wheels that cut front-end bounce in half . . . and the most restful shock-absorbing seat ever put on a tractor—these are just a few of many extra-value features you'll find in the new 4-plow "620" Tractor, shown above with John Deere Four-Row, Quik-Tatch Cultivator.*

Investigate the liberal John Deere Credit Plan—the easy, convenient means of paying for a new tractor while it earns profits for you.

6 Power Sizes... 30 Basic Models

Every One Is NEW...in Looks...in Performance...in Value

"370" SERIES   "420" SERIES   "520" SERIES   "620" SERIES   "720" SERIES   "820" DIESEL

JOHN DEERE

"WHEREVER CROPS GROW, THERE'S A GROWING DEMAND FOR JOHN DEERE FARM EQUIPMENT"

96

1958
MODEL 820

Topping John Deere's 20-series model line was the mighty 820. It evolved from the Model 80, and except for its yellow hood stripes and wider fenders, looked nearly identical to its predecessor.

Weighing in at nearly four tons, the 820 was powered by a 471-cubic-inch two-cylinder diesel started by a gasoline-fueled "pony" motor.

At first the diesel produced about 68 horsepower, but later 1958 models received modifications that boosted the figure to a whopping 75.6 horsepower. These later versions also sported a black dashboard, and are thus known to collectors as "Black-dash 820s"; earlier models, such as the one pictured, had a body-colored dash. In both cases, the dashboard was beginning to look very

carlike, with gauges spread horizontally across a wide panel.

With its six-speed transmission placed in high gear, the 820 could sprint along at more than 12 mph, but its intended use was to pull up to six plows through the toughest soil. It was succeeded after only two years by the nearly identical 830, and these tractors represented the pinnacle of John Deere's "Two cylinder" era.

STEP UP to New Farming Ease and Convenience with a New **JOHN DEERE Tractor**

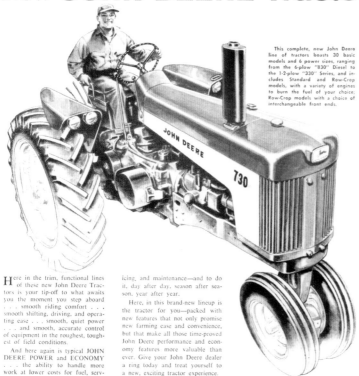

This complete, new John Deere line of tractors boasts 30 basic models and 6 power sizes, ranging from the 6-plow "830" Diesel to the 1-2-plow "330" Series, and includes Standard and Row-Crop models, with a variety of engines to burn the fuel of your choice; Row-Crop models with a choice of interchangeable front ends.

Here in the trim, functional lines of these new John Deere Tractors is your tip-off to what awaits you the moment you step aboard . . . smooth riding comfort . . . smooth shifting, driving, and operating ease . . . smooth, quiet power . . . and smooth, accurate control of equipment in the roughest, toughest of field conditions.

And here again is typical JOHN DEERE POWER and ECONOMY . . . the ability to handle more work at lower costs for fuel, serv-

icing, and maintenance—and to do it, day after day, season after season, year after year.

Here, in this brand-new lineup is the tractor for you—packed with new features that not only promise new farming ease and convenience, but that make all those time-proved John Deere performance and economy features more valuable than ever. Give your John Deere dealer a ring today and treat yourself to a new, exciting tractor experience.

"WHEREVER CROPS GROW, THERE'S A GROWING DEMAND FOR JOHN DEERE FARM EQUIPMENT"

1959
MODEL 330

Acting as John Deere's "entry level" tractor in the late 1950s was the Model 330, a close descendent of the Model 320 that had been introduced for 1956. Both models featured a vertical two-cylinder engine (as did the larger 420/430), a remnant of the Model M of the late 1940s. Offered only in a gasoline-fueled version, it displaced 100.5 cubic inches and produced about 21 horsepower. Its four-speed transmission allowed a top speed of 12 mph.

Tipping the scales at less than 3000 pounds and priced just over $2000, the 330 was often used as a small utility tractor. But the ad at left proclaims it a "1-2 plow tractor," so it could also do conventional farm work, making it the perfect choice for smaller acreages. Like all of

John Deere's 30-series tractors, the 330 featured an angled steering wheel, which most farmers found more comfortable than the former vertical placement.

Despite low sales numbers compared with other Deeres of the period—or perhaps because of them—the 330 has since become a prized tractor in collector circles.

Get
Double
Satisfaction
at
PLOWING TIME

The economical John Deere "530" works well with the 810A 3-bottom Moldboard Plow.

JOHN DEERE 530

...*Choose a* **JOHN DEERE** *Plow* _and_ *Tractor*

Here's a plowing team that assures top-notch, thorough soil conditioning . . . that makes crop-boosting seedbeds for bigger, better yields . . . and does it fast and economically. It's a John Deere Plow behind a John Deere Tractor.

Check the many qualities of John Deere drawn and integral plows Truss-Frame design for strength, rigidity, and full three-way trash-shedding clearance . . . high-speed, light-draft bottoms with low-cost shares for fast, good, economical work . . . "line of draft" hitching for efficient power use . . . wide range of precise, positive

adjustment . . . easy handling . . . long life with low upkeep cost.

Check also the outstanding performance of John Deere Tractors their husky lugging power and peak fuel economy. Enjoy *Advanced* Power Steering and precision hydraulic control. Profit from their versatile 3-point hitch with exclusive Load-and-Depth Control that matches traction to the load *automatically* . . . contributes to a more uniform plowing job and to more acres worked each day. Ask your dealer for a demonstration of a profitable John Deere plowing team.

You've never seen a handier, more efficient plowing team than this John Deere "430" Row-Crop Utility with matched, 3-bottom, integral plow.

JOHN DEERE

"WHEREVER CROPS GROW THERE'S A GROWING DEMAND FOR JOHN DEERE FARM EQUIPMENT"

SEND FOR FREE LITERATURE

JOHN DEERE • MOLINE, ILLINOIS • DEPT. B8

Please send me further information on the ☐ "530," "630," "730" Tractors ☐ "430" General-Purpose Tractors ☐ Moldboard Plows ☐ John Deere Credit Plan.

Name _____ ☐ Student

Rural Route _____ *Box* _____

Town _____

State _____

1959
MODEL 430

As was the case for most other models in the 30-series line, the Model 430 looked little different than its 20-series predecessor, the Model 420. Also like the 420, the 430 was sold for just a couple of model years. Distinguishing the two were the 430's wider yellow trim band on the hood, Float Ride seat, and black-painted dashboard, and some versions carried revised rear fenders.

The 430 was offered in seven variations, including a tracked crawler, making it a very versatile tractor. It shared much with the smaller Model 330, but featured a larger, more powerful 113-cubic-inch (vs. 100 cubic inch) vertical two-cylinder engine that came in versions

that ran on gasoline, all-fuel, or Liquid Propane Gas (LPG). Since it had more horsepower and was available in more variations than its smaller sibling while being priced just a bit higher, the 430 far outsold the 330.

In the ad pictured, the 430 (bottom) forfeits top billing to its Model 530 stablemate, which was powered by John Deere's tra-ditional horizontal two-cylinder engine, but it shows both pulling a three-bottom plow. The caption describing the 430 proclaims, "You've never seen a handier, more efficient plowing team than this John Deere 430 Row-Crop Utility with matched, 3-bottom, integral plow." Which was a more glowing assessment than was given to its 530 sibling.

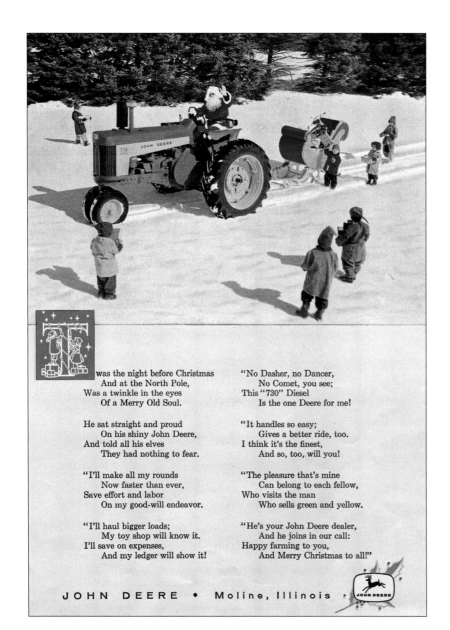

'Twas the night before Christmas
    And at the North Pole,
Was a twinkle in the eyes
    Of a Merry Old Soul.

He sat straight and proud
    On his shiny John Deere,
And told all his elves
    They had nothing to fear.

"I'll make all my rounds
    Now faster than ever,
Save effort and labor
    On my good-will endeavor.

"I'll haul bigger loads;
    My toy shop will know it.
I'll save on expenses,
    And my ledger will show it!

"No Dasher, no Dancer,
    No Comet, you see;
This "730" Diesel
    Is the one Deere for me!

"It handles so easy;
    Gives a better ride, too.
I think it's the finest,
    And so, too, will you!

"The pleasure that's mine
    Can belong to each fellow,
Who visits the man
    Who sells green and yellow.

"He's your John Deere dealer,
    And he joins in our call:
Happy farming to you,
    And Merry Christmas to all!"

JOHN DEERE • Moline, Illinois

1959
MODEL 730

Most John Deere fans would agree that the Model 730 was among the company's most notable offerings. Not only is it considered a "working collectible" today, but it enjoyed tremendous popularity when new, and ended up surviving well past the time John Deere's other two-cylinder models were put to rest.

The 730 was a versatile workhorse, and on many farms, still is today. It was sold with standard, row-crop, and single-wheel front ends, along with a high-crop version. It was John Deere's largest offering save for the 820, which came only with a standard front end. Its 375.6-cubic-inch horizontal two-cylinder engine came in versions that could run on gasoline, all-fuel, or Liquid Propane Gas (LPG), and a larger 375.6-cubic-inch diesel was also available.

Like others in the 30-series line, the 730 carried a different paint scheme than its 20-series pre-decessor, the 720, with a wider yellow trim band underlining the hood. The steering wheel was set at a more convenient angle, as was the dashboard face.

While production of other models in the 30-series line was discontinued in February 1960, the 730 carried on into the summer of that year, and those destined for export to other countries were built until the spring of 1961. After that, parts were shipped to Brazil, where production continued into 1968.

1960
MODEL 630

As was the case with John Deere's other 30-series tractors, the 630 was more of an improved version of its predecessor—in this case, the 620—than an all new design.
The 303-cubic-inch engine carried over in a choice of
gasoline and all-fuel versions, and an LPG-fueled vari-
ant with a cylindrical fuel tank was also offered, all with
ratings of about 50 horsepower. However, a new oval
muffler helped quiet the distinctive exhaust note.

Like its 30-series siblings, the 630 featured a new
paint scheme with more prominent yellow side trim.
The steering wheel and dashboard angled upward for
greater convenience, and the latter held a starter button
to replace the floor pedal used previously. Flat-top fend-

ers could hold four head-
lights and a radio; rounded
"clamshell" fenders were
optional. Other options
included a Float-Ride seat
that could be fitted with
padded armrests.

The 630 was built for
only two years, and this
1960 example closed out
the line. It would prove to
be the last of the legend-
ary two-cylinder John
Deeres, and thus the final
edition of the beloved
"Johnny Poppers."

In *New Generation* JOHN DEERE ENGINES...

bigger, heavier rotating parts follow through where others stall out

Farming with a New Generation Tractor, you'll move through big jobs without hesitation . . . rarely, if ever, shifting down to work through tough spots. Here's why: traditionally heavy John Deere rotating parts, shown in the "4010" Diesel engine cutaway, build up tremendous energy (a reserve of power) for real lugging ability. Note the larger pistons, heavier connecting rods,

bigger-diameter piston pins, and massive crankshaft (150 lbs.)—backed by a heavy flywheel and clutch assembly. Put this beefy engine assembly into motion and it just "plain and simple" doesn't like to be stopped!

Another thing, John Deere builds this engine to "deliver" dependably over many seasons of hard use. The "4010" crankshaft, for example, is carried on seven main bearings in a solid foundation to "stay put" under the most extreme loads.

These advantages, together with dozens of other advanced features, make a John Deere New Generation Tractor your best buy for efficient, dependable, trouble-free farming power. Your John Deere dealer has a type and power size to fit your needs exactly.

JOHN DEERE · 3300 RIVER DRIVE, MOLINE, ILL.

Arrange for an on-your-farm demonstration of a New Generation 35 h.p. "1010," 45 h.p. "2010," 55 h.p. "3010," or 80 h.p. "4010." Contact your John Deere dealer today. Ask about his liberal John Deere Credit Plan, too.

JOHN DEERE
125 YEARS

JOHN DEERE design, dependability, and dealers **MAKE THE DIFFERENCE**

1963
MODEL 4010

To John Deere traditionalists, the New Generation models introduced in October 1960 came as quite a shock. Many couldn't believe the company would forsake the two-cylinder arrangement that had always been John Deere's trademark—and greatest selling point.

But only so much power can be efficiently wrung from two cylinders, and John Deere had maxed out the design's potential. With farmers asking for more, the company needed to head in a new direction.

The first New Generation John Deere to hit the fields was the 4010—destined to be the biggest in the initial lineup. Power came from an inline six-cylinder (gasp!) engine, with gasoline, LPG, and diesel versions offering

up to 75 horsepower. Standard and row-crop front ends were available, as was a hi-crop variation.

Not only was the 4010 more powerful than any of its predecessors, it also introduced some new features, such as an eight-speed transmission, an innovative central hydraulic system, and an orthopedist-designed seat that became a benchmark for comfort.

NEW in JOHN DEERE
3020 and 4020 TRACTORS

Powershift
STRAIGHT THROUGH
WITHOUT CLUTCHING

Change gears under full load...shift freely and instantly to any of the eight forward and four reverse selections without any interruption of power to the drive wheels. Do it on the go; do it without touching the clutch! This is the new John Deere Power Shift Transmission—and it's a honey! Hydraulic power makes speed selection almost effortless; in fact, it's enjoyable.

Now, you can shift up or down quickly to match soil conditions on tillage operations. You'll upshift to sprint across headlands; drop back to your work gear without hesitation. A flip of the shifter lever maintains the proper ground speed to keep PTO equipment working at full capacity without clogging. Heavy loads can be started in a power gear and moved smoothly and swiftly up to top transport speeds. On downgrades or at row ends, you

can shift back and slow down in a jiffy—and you enjoy the added security of positive hold-back action in all gears. Power Shift also provides direction-reverser action, again without clutching. Summed up, Power Shift will save a big slice of your time and effort and provide you with the most efficient control ever over tractor power.

New John Deere "3020" and "4020" Tractors are available with either new Power Shift or Syncro-Range Transmission. Both transmissions provide a fine selection of realistic speeds matched to your every job. Both are real huskies—fully capable of taking full advantage of the higher horsepower of the new tractors. Make a date soon to experience the tremendous field performance of a new "3020" or "4020" Tractor equipped with the transmission of your choice.

1965
MODEL 4020

Despite some initial misgivings, the New Generation John Deeres introduced in 1960 met with almost universal acclaim. The 4010 had made a name for itself as the top-line model, but Deere soon decided some detail-tweaking was in order.

Still fitted with the inline-six first used in the 4010, the 4020 delivered even more power. Gasoline or LPG fed a 340-cubic-inch engine, while the diesel measured 404 cubic inches. Two transmissions were offered, both with eight speeds: the standard Syncro-Range, or the easier-to-use Powershift, which allowed shifting without using the clutch. In top gear, a 4020 could zip along at nearly 19 mph.

Row-crop, standard, and hi-crop versions were offered, with base prices spanning a range of $4714 to $5366 in 1965. A protective cab was available as an option.

As opposed to its immediate predecessors, the 4020 enjoyed a relatively long production run, the final examples rolling off the line in 1972. Many of these tractors are still in use today, and they often cost more on the used market than they did when new.

New 5020 Row-Crop Tractor...
132 h.p....world's most powerful

You're equipped to produce a lot more groceries, and show a better net profit, with a new 132 h.p. "5020" Row-Crop. It widens the measure of your ability as it tightens the belt on your production costs.

Think Big—You'll plow with 8 bottoms at a steady 4-1/2 mph . . . finish fields faster, at lower cost, than you could with two 4-plow tractors.

Hook onto an 8-row minimum-tillage rig . . . plant in 30-inch rows . . . cut trips over the field 50 percent. You'll require fewer fairweather Spring days to complete planting. Cultivate as many rows with a "5020" Row-Crop in one pass as you did in two or three trips before. With a 1,000 rpm forage harvester powered by a new "5020,"

you'll chop—even recut—two heavy-as-they-come rows non-stop.

It's unbeatable—The "5020's" variable-speed 6-cylinder Diesel works hand-in-hand with the 8 overlapping speed ranges of the Syncro-Range Transmission. A speed for every need is supplied—from a 1-1/2 mph crawl for powershaft work to a rapid transport 20 mph. You're in finger-

tip command of hydraulic power for steering, braking, implement control, PTO and differential-lock operation. And the new "5020" Row-Crop has more tractive weight than any other over-100 h.p. row-crop tractor. Yet it treads lightly as it delivers big-tool pulling power to drive wheels. Here's why:

New Rear-Wheel Option: Double

rear wheels, shown above, are individually adjustable on the axle. Set them in for plowing . . . space them to straddle rows for cultivating . . . or drop off the outer wheel for rebedding. Each securely fastened, heavy, cast wheel can transmit full horsepower.

Seize the opportunity . . . field-test a "5020" Row-Crop soon.

MORE OPPORTUNITIES NEXT PAGE

1966
MODEL 5020

With the advent of John Deere's New Generation six-cylinder engines, power reached unprecedented levels. The diesel in the mid-'60s 5020 churned out 132 horses from 531.6 cubic inches, enough to lay claim in contemporary ads to being the "world's most powerful."

Initially, the 5020 came only with a standard front end, but a row-crop version was added in 1967, making the big tractor even more versatile. Options included a cab with heater and air conditioning, remote hydraulics with single or double output, and a three-point hitch with Quik-Coupler and live PTO.

An eight-speed Syncro-Range transmission provided speeds from 1½ mph to 20 mph, and ads stated the 5020

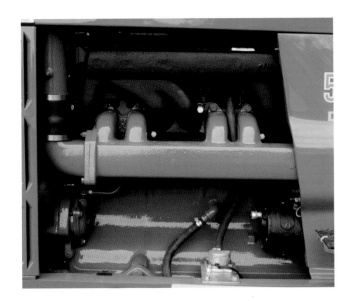

could "plow with 8 bottoms at a steady 4½ mph"—a valuable asset to many farmers, as they'd need "fewer fair-weather Spring days to complete planting." Indeed, the 5020 could do twice the work of many large tractors built just ten years before, and in the hands of an able farmer, would become a significant contributor to the food baskets of the world.